Kingfisher first thesaurus

KINGFISHER

KINGFISHER

Kingfisher Publications Plc
New Penderel House
283–288 High Holborn
London WC1V 7HZ
www.kingfisherpub.com

First published in 1993 by Kingfisher Publications Plc
This edition first published in 2005
10 9 8 7 6 5 4 3 2 1

1TR/1104/TWP/PICA/150ENSOMA

A CIP catalogue record for this book
is available from the British Library

ISBN-13: 978 0 7534 1131 5
ISBN-10: 0 7534 1131 8

Printed in Singapore

Introduction

The word *Thesaurus* is from the Greek for 'treasury', and that indeed is what it is – a rich treasury of words from which you can pick and choose at will.

In this thesaurus we have selected over one hundred commonly used words and listed with them other words with similar meanings (the technical word for another word with a similar meaning is *synonym*). If you look up 'pick', for instance, you will be given four other words: choose, gather, pluck, select. Wouldn't it be much easier, you may ask, if we had only one word for each idea or object? Here is an example with 'nice', a very commonly over-used word!

After their **nice** supper, the kittens went to sleep on a **nice** cushion. It was then that I considered how **nice** it was of that **nice** woman next door to offer to look after them when we are away having a **nice** time. We must buy her a **nice** present, perhaps a **nice** straw hat so that she can have a **nice** time sitting in her **nice** garden.

Doesn't that sound flat and repetitious with all those **nices**? Here is an alternative version:

After their **delicious** supper, the kittens went to sleep on a **comfortable** cushion. It was then that I considered how **thoughtful** it was of that **kind** woman next door to look after them when we are away having an **enjoyable** time. We must buy her a **super** present, perhaps a **smart** straw hat so that she can have a **pleasant** time sitting in her **lovely** garden.

So you see it is worth looking for the exact word to give life to what you are trying to say.

It is important to remember that the lists we give are words of *similar* meaning, for there are few words which mean exactly the same as another. Take the word 'fast' for instance. It means almost the same as 'quick', yet we would speak of a 'fast car' or a 'fast train' but not of a 'quick car' or a 'quick train'. That is why we provide sample sentences to show how to use the word correctly.

A thesaurus is a fascinating word-finder, a source book, a priceless treasury which shows the marvellous variety and richness of the English language. English more than any other language has borrowed words from all around the world and absorbed and anglicized them. Onto the plain and simple tongue of the Anglo-Saxons has been added a vast hoard of Latin and Norman French words – so that the Old English 'forgive', 'gift', and 'give' are matched by 'pardon', 'present', and 'donate' from Latin and Norman French. Thousands of words stem from Greek, the language of learning. Where would we be without electronics, phones, oxygen, and electricity? From the Germans we get dachshunds, hamburgers, and kindergartens. To Turkey we owe divans, kiosks, tulips, and yoghurt. To Spain we are grateful for siestas, canteens, and guerillas. The Arabs provide us with cotton, syrup, sofas, and mattresses, the Dutch with brandy, landscapes, sleighs, wagons, and yachts. And so on around the world.

We hope you derive hours of pleasure

from browsing through your thesaurus and that you will discover the joy and satisfaction of writing a letter or story or whatever, and conveying what you want to say exactly and interestingly.

How to use your thesaurus

All the 'entry' words that appear in this thesaurus are in alphabetical order, for example: **bar, bashful, battle, bear, beat,** and so on. When we reach one of the 'keywords' an arrow points to a panel, which is usually illustrated. (We shall explain what the panel contains in a moment.) All words that are not key-words tell you to look up another word, which is usually a keyword and some-times the opposite of a keyword. If you look up 'acquaintance' it will say 'see friend'; 'arrive' will tell you to look up 'come and the opposite of leave'.

The panels of keywords contain other words with similar meanings. So under 'beautiful' are its synonyms: fair, hand-some, lovely, pretty.

The keyword 'beautiful' is followed by its part of speech in italic type (*adjective*).

The word is then defined as it would be in a dictionary: 'Something we enjoy looking at, or someone who is very good-looking or attractive, is described as beautiful.' This is followed by at least one example of how the word 'beautiful' can be used.

Each synonym is followed by a sample sentence. Sometimes we add a further list of 'other words' but without sample sentences. Under 'beautiful' we list cute, gorgeous, splendid, and sweet.

Where they exist, we give the opposite words (antonyms). If the opposite word is also a keyword we simply say 'see such and such a word'. If the opposite word is not a keyword we add a sample sentence.

Where there is a word with the same sound as the keyword (a homonym) we include it with a sample sentence. For example under 'break' the 'same sound' word is 'brake', followed by a sentence.

Topic pages

An important feature of this thesaurus are the special, highly illustrated topic features. The topics range from animals, houses, and music to sport, travel, and weather. These pages contain such things as different groups – river, brook, stream, burn; guitar, violin, cello – word games, palindromes, homonyms, rhymes, and limericks. They are inten-ded to help you extend your vocabulary and to add a bit of fun.

A

abandon
see leave

able

able *(adjective)*

You are **able** to do something if you are good at it, or are well enough to do it: *If I go to France, I will be **able** to speak French, because I learned it at school.*

capable   Our teacher is **capable** of making us laugh; she's very funny.

deft   Jo is so **deft** with her pocket-knife, she has carved a pattern on that stick.

skilful   My mother is **skilful** – a brilliant artist and a wonderful teacher.

strong   Elephants are **strong** enough to lift whole tree trunks.

talented   What a **talented** family! Steve plays the violin, and Mary plays the piano.

Opposite word

unskilled   The table fell apart because it was made by **unskilled** workers.

about

ache
see hurt

acquaintance
see friend

adjust
see change

admirable
see good

admire
see like

adore
see love

affect
see touch

affection
see love

afraid

aged
see old

agree
see say

aid
see help

aim
see try

about *(adverb)*

When you use the word **about**, it is usually because you are not certain exactly: *It's **about** time we started. We went to Bermuda **about** six months ago.*

almost   It's **almost** twelve o'clock; we must hurry to catch the train.

nearly   This piece of cloth is **nearly** the right length.

around   *(preposition)* Wherever we went, there were flowers all **around** us.

afraid *(adjective)*

When you think something nasty may happen or if you are full of fear, you can often use the word **afraid**: *When I was very little, I was **afraid** of the dark.*

frightened   Who's **frightened** of ghosts?

nervous   Henry was **nervous** about going to the dentist.

scared   Don't be **scared**; the bull only looks fierce.

Opposite words *see* bold

airy
  see light

alarm
  see fright

almost
  see about

alone
  see lonely

alter
  see change

amusing
  see funny

ancient
  see old

angry

answer
  see opposite
  of ask

antique
  see old

appear
  see come

approach
  see come

angry *(adjective)*

If someone annoys you or is rude to you, you are likely to be **angry**: *We got quite **angry** when we saw the children scaring the sheep.*

cross	Mark was really **cross** when Anne won the game.
furious	Dan is **furious** when I'm late.
indignant	Sarah was **indignant** when Pete accused her of telling lies.
irate	The **irate** farmer shook her fist at the hiker who left the gate open.
mad	My mother was **mad** at me when I smashed the window.
upset	Jill was **upset** when Adam rode his bike over her foot.

Other words annoyed, irritable, worked up

Opposite words

friendly	Keith gave me a **friendly** smile.
pleased	I was **pleased** with the photo.

All about animals

Birds fly

Animal movements

Kittens pounce

Frogs hop

Deer leap

Kangaroos bound

Cheetahs run

Fish swim

Caterpillars creep

Kinds of animal

Mammals give birth to live young which they suckle with milk. They include humans, dogs, elephants, kangaroos (known as marsupials), and sea mammals such as whales and dolphins.

Reptiles include snakes, lizards, tortoises, and crocodiles. In prehistoric times reptiles ruled the Earth.

Insects are the most numerous of all the different kinds of animal. They live all over the world.

Spiders Unlike all insects, spiders have eight legs. All spiders spin silk threads.

Amphibians are animals such as frogs, toads, and newts. Most start their lives in water.

Birds developed from reptiles. All birds lay eggs. Some birds, such as the kiwi, cannot fly.

Fish were the first animals with backbones (vertebrates) to develop on Earth. Fish breathe through gills.

Animal terms

animal	group	male	female	young
donkey	herd	jackass	jenny	foal
badger	cete	boar	sow	cub
cat	litter	tom	queen	kitten
cattle	herd	bull	cow	calf
dog	pack	dog	bitch	pup
fox	skulk	dog	vixen	cub
goat	herd	billy	nanny	kid
goose	flock	goose	gander	gosling
horse	herd	stallion	mare	foal
				filly (female)
				colt (male)
lion	pride	lion	lioness	cub
pig	herd	boar	sow	piglet
seal	colony	bull	cow	pup
sheep	flock	ram	ewe	lamb
whale	school	bull	cow	calf

Animal homes

Tigers live in the jungle.

Hippopotamuses live in rivers.

Frogs live in ponds.

Bats live in caves.

Camels live in deserts.

Whales live in the sea.

Animal sounds

Bees *buzz*

Cats *miaow*

Cockerels *crow*

Cows *moo*

Crows *caw*

Dogs *bark*

Ducks *quack*

Horses *neigh*

Lions *roar*

Mice *squeak*

Owls *hoot*

Pigs *grunt*

Snakes *hiss*

Wolves *howl*

arid
see dry *and*
opposite of wet

around
see about

arrest
see catch

arrive
see come *and*
opposite of leave

ascend
see rise

ask

assist
see help

attempt
see try

average
see fair

awful
see hard

ask *(verb)*

To **ask**, you speak in order to get information about something: *If you want to find out about stamps, then **ask** a philatelist.*

beg   The defendant **begged** the judge not to send her to prison.

demand   *To order or require*: I **demand** more money.

enquire   *To ask questions*: May I **enquire** what time it is?

invite   *To ask someone to do something*: Ian **invited** me to his party.

query   "What's your name?" he **queried**.

request   She **requested** us to stand up.

Opposite word

answer   Will you **answer** my questions?

B

bad

bake
see cook

bar
see shut

barbecue
see cook

bashful
*see opposite
of* bold

battle
see fight

bad *(adjective)*

When something is not good, or is wrong or harmful, we say that it is **bad**: *Sue's writing is so **bad**, I find it hard to read. They say that we shall have **bad** weather tomorrow.*

dangerous
This road is not safe; there are many **dangerous** corners.

disagreeable
We didn't enjoy the party; the guests were so **disagreeable**.

evil
The demon looks **evil**.

nasty
My mother scolded me for being **nasty** to my brother.

naughty
Ill-behaved or disobedient: Michael was very **naughty**; he pulled the cat's tail.

rotten
Spoiled, or poor in quality: All the fruit was **rotten**.

sour
We couldn't use the milk as it had gone **sour**.

Other words harmful, horrible, horrid, mischievous, repulsive, vile, wicked

Opposite words *see* good

bear
see take

beat
see hit

beautiful

become
see get, grow

beg
see ask

begin
see start

believe
see think

bend
see turn

bestow
see give

beautiful *(adjective)*

Something we enjoy looking at, or someone who is very good-looking or attractive, is described as **beautiful**: *My mother is wearing a* **beautiful** *hat. It was such a* **beautiful** *day that we went to the beach.*

fair   Cinderella was **fairer** than her step-sisters.

handsome The black horse was a truly **handsome** creature.

lovely   These flowers are **lovely**.

pretty   I think pink is a **pretty** colour.

Other words cute, gorgeous, splendid, sweet

Opposite word

ugly   Some deep-sea fish look really **ugly**.

big

bit
see piece

blank
see empty

blend
see mix

blond(e)
see fair

big *(adjective)*

Something is called **big** because it is sizeable or important: *Canada is a very **big** country, although it does not have a large population.*

enormous	Jumbo jets are **enormous**.
great	*Famous or prominent:* 'Babe' Ruth was one of America's **great** baseball players.
heavy	In the old days **heavy**, unwieldy steam engines pulled trains.
huge	The giant has **huge** muscles.
large	Paris and Rio are **large** cities.
vast	The desert is too **vast** to cross.
wide	The **wide** lorry can't go down this narrow street.

Other words adult, colossal, gigantic

Opposite words

little	There was **little** hope of finding the missing aircraft.
small	That hole is **small** enough for a mouse to get through.
tiny	Ants have **tiny** feet.

blunt
  see dull

boil
  see cook

boisterous
  see loud, rough

bold

bolt
  see escape

boring
  see dull

boundary
  see end

brainy
  see clever

brave
  see bold

brawny
  see strong

bold *(adjective)*

Bold people face danger without fear: *The early explorers were **bold**, unafraid of the unknown.*

brave
The **brave** firefighters ran up a ladder to the window.

courageous
Sharon was **courageous** in rescuing the cat from the tree.

daring
Martha was **daring** enough to climb the steeple.

Other words adventurous, heroic, rude

Same sound

bowled
The batter was **bowled** out.

Opposite words

bashful
Susan is so **bashful**; she never speaks until spoken to.

shy
Chris is **shy** with new people.

timid
Lacking in confidence: Jo's too **timid** to pat the horse.

break

bright
see clear

bring
see get, take

build
see make

bump
see hit

buoyant
see light

bury
see hide

break *(verb)*

When you **break** something, it comes apart, falls to pieces, or stops working: *Be careful you don't **break** the eggs!*

crack — Don't **crack** nuts with your teeth!

fracture — *If we break a bone, we fracture it*: Al **fractured** his arm in the gym.

shatter — *To break into tiny pieces*: The ball hit the window, and the glass **shattered**.

smash — *To hit something, making it break*: I **smashed** two cups and saucers.

split — Sue **split** the logs in two.

Same sound

brake — The car **braked** at the crossing.

Opposite words

fix — *To put together, or repair*: Sue **fixed** the broken plate with glue.

mend — I must **mend** my faulty brakes.

repair — I'll soon **repair** this old clock.

C

call *(verb)*

We **call** when we cry out, either for help or simply to attract attention: *Will you call me early tomorrow morning? I have to catch a train.*

cry My little brother started to **cry** when dad went to work.

name I'll **name** the cat 'Tiddles'.

shout She **shouted** at her dog to stop.

telephone I'll **telephone** you to say when I can call on you.

visit I'll **visit** my relatives when I go home.

yell Our team scored first, and the fans **yelled** with delight.

calm *(adjective)*

It is **calm** when things are quiet and un-troubled: *After the terrible storm, the wind dropped and all was* **calm** *once more.*

peaceful At night the woods are very noisy, not at all **peaceful**!

placid Joe's an excitable man, but his wife is quiet and **placid**.

still We lay very **still** in the long grass, watching the lions.

see also quiet

Opposite words

disturbed I had a **disturbed** night's sleep; my neighbours had a party.

stormy We can't go sky-diving in this **stormy** weather.

capable
see able

capture
see catch, take

careful

careful *(adjective)*

If we take care and pay attention to what we are doing, we are **careful**: *My grandfather is a careful driver, always aware of other drivers.*

cautious   Be **cautious** on that mountain; there are some steep slopes.

wary   The deer were **wary** of us riding through the forest.

watchful   We were **watchful** as the boat approached the rocky shore.

Opposite words

careless   Tina's work is **careless**; she needs to try harder.

forgetful   Jim's so **forgetful**, he thought it was Wednesday.

rash   Annie is so **rash**; she never thinks what might happen!

thoughtless   Bill has left the door open; he's so **thoughtless**.

careless
*see opposite
of* careful

carry
see take

catch

catch *(verb)*

When we **catch** something, we stop it and get hold of it: *We went out in a boat to **catch** fish.*

arrest   Two police officers **arrested** the thief.

capture   After the lion escaped, it took three hours to **capture** it.

grab   The crane **grabbed** the rubble.

seize   The fox **seized** the lamb in its mouth.

Other words grasp, snatch

Opposite word

release   The war was over, and it was time to **release** all prisoners.

cautious

cautious
see careful

certain
see sure

change

chat
see talk

cheerful
see happy *and*
opposite of sad

chew
see eat

change *(verb)*

You **change** something if you make it different or put something in its place: *I'll **change** my clothes before dinner.*

adjust   You can **adjust** the height of the chair.

alter   I'll **alter** the room by replacing the wallpaper.

exchange   I had a yellow hat but I **exchanged** it for a blue one.

modify   The car cost too much to make, so they had to **modify** it.

swap   I collect Australian stamps and **swap** Canadian ones for them.

vary   Dogs **vary** in size from Irish wolfhounds to Chihuahuas.

see also turn

Other words amend, convert, replace, revise, transform

Opposite words

conserve   We've **conserved** the house's Colonial-style exterior.

retain   Rita **retains** her old name.

chilly
see cold

choose
see pick

chop
see cut

chuckle
see laugh

clamour
see noise

clean
see opposite
of dirty

clear

clear *(adjective)*

If something is easy to see through, or without obstacles, we say it is **clear**: *It was a lovely day; the sky was **clear** and cloudless. The answer to the problem is **clear**.*

bright   A **bright** beam shone on the car.

obvious   *Plain to see*:
We're lost; it's **obvious** we've taken the wrong turning.

plain   It's **plain** you've got mumps.

pure   The glass contained **pure** water.

simple   There is no **simple** answer to such a complicated question.

see also empty, plain

Opposite words

dim   The lights on my bike are **dim** because the battery is low.

misty   It's too **misty** to see the tower.

see also dull

clever

clever

clip
see cut

close
see shut

closed
see shut

clumsy
see opposite
of clever

clutch
see hold

clutter
see mess

clever *(adjective)*

People who are **clever** are sharp-witted and have a quick mind: *Debbie is really **clever**; she'll probably become a professor at least!*

brainy   Isaac was so **brainy**, he could count when he was three!

cunning   Foxes are **cunning** and sly.

intelligent   My dog is very **intelligent**; she can do 20 different tricks.

talented   Yehudi Menuhin was a **talented** boy. He could play the violin in concerts when he was seven.

see also able

Opposite words

clumsy   Dick will never learn to dance; he's even **clumsy** when he walks.

stupid   Our parrot can't speak a single word; she's too **stupid**!

see also dull

22

coarse
see rough

cold

collect
see get

combat
see fight

combine
see mix

cold *(adjective)*

When the temperature gets low, we say it is **cold**: *The weather in Siberia is very* **cold**.

chilly   I need more blankets on my bed; the room was **chilly** last night.

cool   After the heat of summer, it's nice to have a few **cool** breezes.

freezing   The water on the pond is **freezing**. Let's go skating.

Other words crisp, frosty, icy, nippy

Opposite word

hot   The Sun had heated the sand, making it too **hot** to sit on.

The community's helping hands

Teachers and professors help us to learn.

Doctors make sick people better.

Firefighters put out fires and rescue people.

Postwomen and postmen deliver our mail.

Rubbish collectors take away our garbage.

Dentists look after our teeth.

Other words for teacher
coach   head teacher   schoolmaster   schoolmistress
instructor   lecturer   professor   trainer   tutor

Ambulance drivers take the sick and injured to hospital.

Priests and rabbis advise and console people.

Nurses look after the sick.

Cooks prepare meals.

The police help keep us safe.

Bus and train drivers take us to school and work.

Match the people above with these places:
church   synagogue   fire station   hospital   school
post office   kitchen   police station   railway station

come

comfortable
see nice

comical
see funny

commence
see start

companion
see friend

compel
see make

complete
see full

complicated
see hard *and*
opposite of plain

comrade
see friend

conceal
see hide

conclude
see end, think

confident
see sure

come *(verb)*

If you move towards someone, they will say that you have **come**: *Uncle Bill has just **come** from South America.*

appear	I went out to meet Jenny, and she **appeared** at the end of the street.
approach	A police officer **approached** our car to warn us of an accident.
arrive	Guests started to **arrive** at six o'clock.
enter	When you reach the theatre, **enter** by the stage door.
happen	Hanukkah **happens** once a year.
occur	The Sabbath **occurs** every week.

Opposite words *see* go, leave

connect
see join

conserve
see opposite
of change

consider
see think

console
see opposite
of hurt

construct
see make

contain
see hold

contented
see happy

continue
see go, keep

convey
see send

cook

cool
see cold

correct
see right *and*
opposite of wrong

courageous
see bold

cover
see hide

cook *(verb)*

If you **cook** food, you heat it in some way to prepare it for eating: *My father taught me how to cook, and my brother learned too!*

bake   You **bake** cakes in an oven.

barbecue   In summer we **barbecue** food on a fire outside.

boil   **Boil** some water for tea.

fry   We made a fire to **fry** our food.

grill   You **grill** tomatoes without oil.

roast   We **roasted** chestnuts in the fire.

stew   All the apples were put into a pot, and then we **stewed** them.

toast   We **toasted** muffins for tea.

Containers

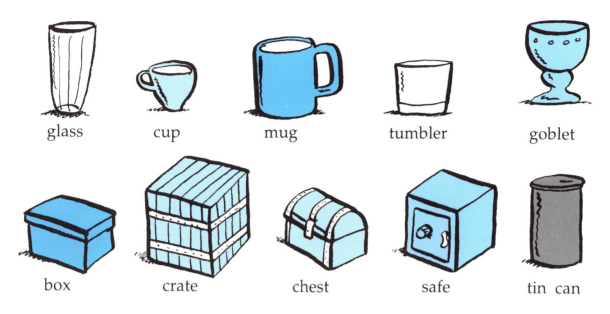

glass   cup   mug   tumbler   goblet

box   crate   chest   safe   tin can

envelope

pocket

Double words

Fill in the missing word in the centre of each line, remembering that the clues on each side refer to it.

pot _ _ _ _ _ _ ship

tin _ _ _ able

bag _ _ _ _ dismiss

basin _ _ _ _ submerge

drawer

vase

aquarium

28

bucket / pail

baggage / luggage

suitcase

trunk

jug

jar

sack

bag

pack

bowl

cone

briefcase

rucksack

sink
basin

flowerpot

flask

basket

wheelbarrow

saucepan

casserole

tray

frying pan

skillet

crack
  see break

cross
  see angry

crude
  see rough

cry
  see call *and*
  opposite of laugh

cunning
  see clever

cut

cut *(verb)*

If you **cut** something, you divide it by using something sharp: *Ben took the scissors and **cut** the card into three pieces.*

chop Margaret **chopped** the logs into firewood with her new axe.

clip Who'll **clip** the hedge?

prune Now's the time to **prune** the roses.

saw I'll **saw** these planks in no time with my new electric saw.

slice If you **slice** the bread, I'll make the sandwiches.

snip I don't need all that parsley. Can you **snip** a little off the bunch?

trim The barber **trimmed** my hair.

D

damage
see hurt

damp
see wet

dangerous
see bad

daring
see bold

dash
see hurry, run

dawdle
see opposite of hurry

declare
see say

decline
see opposite of rise

decrease
see opposite of grow, rise

deft
see able

delay
see opposite of hurry

delicate
see soft, weak, *and opposite of* rough

delicious
see nice

delighted
see happy

demand
see ask

demonstrate
see show

dense
see hard

deny
see opposite of give

depart
see go, leave

deposit
see put

depressed
see sad

descend
see fall *and opposite of* rise

desert
see leave

destroy
see opposite of make

develop
see grow

devour
see eat

difficult
see hard

difficulty
see mess

dim
see opposite of clear

din
see noise

dine
see eat

dirty

disagreeable
see bad

discard
*see opposite
of* keep

disconnect
*see opposite
of* join

discover
see find

discuss
see talk

disguise
see hide

dismal
see sad

dismay
see fright

dispatch
see send

display
see show

distrustful
*see opposite
of* sure

dirty *(adjective)*

If something is not clean, we say that it's **dirty**: *We took our **dirty** towels to the launderette.*

filthy   His glasses are so **filthy**, he can hardly see through them.

foul   The ship's cargo had gone bad, and there was a **foul** smell.

grimy   A hundred years ago, **grimy** urchins begged in the streets.

impure   This water is **impure**. You'll be ill if you drink it.

polluted   The atmosphere is **polluted** with car fumes.

soiled   Her shoes were **soiled** with mud.

Other words shabby, stained, unclean

Opposite word

clean   Have you got a **clean** hanky?

disturbed
  see opposite of calm

disturbing
  see opposite of quiet

donate
  see give

doubtful
  see opposite of sure

drab
  see dull

drag
  see pull

draw
  see pull

drawing
  see picture

drop
  see fall

dry

dry *(adjective)*

When anything is without moisture or wetness, we say that it is **dry**: *We've had such a **dry** summer, there will be a poor harvest.*

arid　　　Parched, **arid** land is caused by drought.

parched　　Let's have a drink. I'm thirsty and my throat is **parched**.

uninteresting　Mark reads such dry books; they look so **uninteresting**.

Other words boring, monotonous, tedious

Opposite words *see* wet

dull *(adjective)*

If something is not very bright or interesting, we can say that it is **dull**: *We switched off the TV because the programmes were so **dull**.*

blunt   My pencil point is **blunt**; can you lend me your sharpener?

boring   They spent the evening playing cards, which I think is **boring**.

drab   When it rains, the **drab** streets look even more miserable.

gloomy   The paper was full of **gloomy** news of wars and disasters.

Other words misty, monotonous, tedious

Opposite words

sharp   That axe won't cut unless it's **sharp**.

see also bright, clear, clever, interesting

E

earn
  see get, make

eat

eat *(verb)*

When we **eat**, we take food into our body: *I like to **eat** ice cream in the summer.*

chew   Our new puppy has just **chewed** my slippers.

devour   Caterpillars have **devoured** the cabbages.

dine   We **dined** at the new Chinese restaurant.

gorge   Nick had stomach ache after he **gorged** all the apples.

nibble   Rabbits **nibble** carrots.

swallow   Harry **swallowed** a fishbone, and it stuck in his throat.

effort
see try, work

employment
see work

empty

empty (adjective)

If something, such as a box, has nothing in it, we say it is **empty**: *Amy drank the milk until the glass was empty.*

blank   Here's a **blank** sheet of paper.

clear   Sweep the path until it's **clear**.

unoccupied   We rang the bell, but the house was **unoccupied**.

vacant   We couldn't stay at the hotel; they had no **vacant** rooms.

void   *(noun)* The planet was uninhabited; it was just a **void**.

see also clear

Opposite words

occupied   The phone box was **occupied**, so we had to wait.

packed   The room was **packed** with people.

see also full

end

enemy
see opposite of friend

enjoyable
see nice

enlarge
see grow

enormous
see big

enquire
see ask

enter
see come

entertaining
see interesting

entire
see full

end *(verb)*

This can be either a *verb*: *We shall* **end** *our meeting this afternoon.* Or it can be a *noun*: *We reached the* **end** *of our journey feeling tired.*

conclude The teachers **concluded** their talk after an hour.

finish The game **finished** at four o'clock.

terminate The train **terminates** here, but you can take a bus to the town.

boundary *(noun)* The river Rhine marks the **boundary** between several countries.

Opposite words *see* start

escape

establish
see start

esteem
see love

even
see smooth *and*
opposite of odd

evil
see bad

excellent
see good

exchange
see change

exclaim
see say

expect
see think

experience
see feel

expose
see show

extend
see grow

escape *(verb)*

When you **escape**, you get away, get free, or get out: *The prisoner's door was locked, but he managed to* **escape** *through the window.*

bolt   The horse **bolted** out of the stable.

flee   The sheep **fled** from the wolf.

scarper   The thieves **scarpered** when the alarm went off.

Opposite words *see* catch

F

faint
see weak

fair

fair *(adjective)*

If you are honest and play by the rules, you can be called **fair**: *Mrs Jones is always fair, and has no favourites.* **Fair** also means having light-coloured hair or skin.

average   It wasn't a great film, only **average**.

blond(e)   My son has wonderful **blond** hair.

just   My father is stern, but **just**.

light   He was pale, with **light** skin.

mediocre   This is a **mediocre** essay; it's really not very good.

reasonable   These prices are **reasonable**.

see also beautiful, light

Same sound

fare   *(noun)* How much is the bus **fare** to the zoo?

Opposite words

fraudulent   It was a **fraudulent** business, selling brass rings as gold ones.

unfair   The referee was **unfair**, and favoured the home team.

fall

fall *(verb)*

Something **falls** if it drops down or becomes lower: *These stairs are so steep, I'm afraid I might fall.*

descend The lift **descended** from the third floor to the first floor.

drop **Drop** a coin in the fountain and make a wish.

sink Soon that submarine will **sink** below the surface.

trip He **tripped** over a stone.

tumble Jill **tumbled** down the hill.

Opposite words *see* rise

false
see wrong *and
opposite of* right

famous
see important

fancy
see think

fascinating
see interesting

fast

fast *(adjective)*

Something that moves at speed can be called **fast**: *We caught a **fast** train and were soon home.* **Fast** can also mean fixed and steady.

firm   She stood there, **firm** as a rock.

quick   I know a **quick** way to the town.

rapid   We crossed the river with a few **rapid** strokes of the oars.

secure   The boat is tied up and **secure**.

swift   It was a **swift** river, with a strong current.

Opposite words

gradual   There has been a **gradual** change in the weather.

slow   Our new car is a bit **slow**.

Family

Everyone is part of a family. If people marry they become part of a new family.

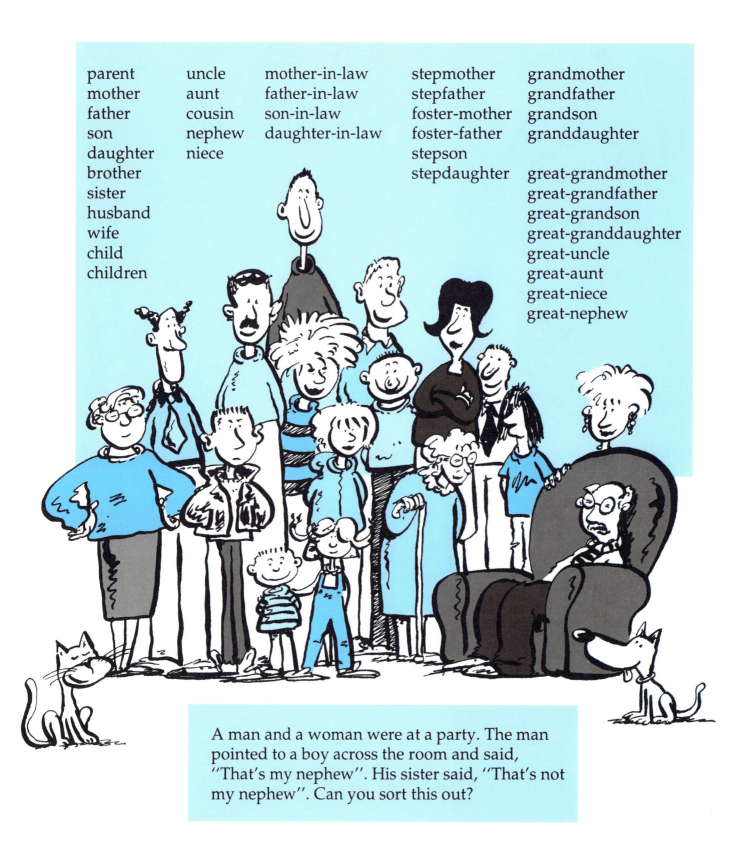

parent
mother
father
son
daughter
brother
sister
husband
wife
child
children

uncle
aunt
cousin
nephew
niece

mother-in-law
father-in-law
son-in-law
daughter-in-law

stepmother
stepfather
foster-mother
foster-father
stepson
stepdaughter

grandmother
grandfather
grandson
granddaughter

great-grandmother
great-grandfather
great-grandson
great-granddaughter
great-uncle
great-aunt
great-niece
great-nephew

A man and a woman were at a party. The man pointed to a boy across the room and said, "That's my nephew". His sister said, "That's not my nephew". Can you sort this out?

Family problems

What relation is . . .

Mr Bowles to his son's daughter?

Mrs Jones to her sister's brother?

Winston to his mother's husband?

Deri to her uncle's son?

Who is your Dad's father?

Monday's child is fair of face,

Tuesday's child is full of grace,

Wednesday's child is full of woe,

Thursday's child has far to go,

Friday's child is loving and giving,

Saturday's child works hard for a living,

And the child that is born on the Sabbath day

Is bonny and blithe, and good and gay.

Solomon Grundy,

Born on Monday,

Christened on Tuesday,

Married on Wednesday,

Took ill on Thursday,

Worse on Friday,

Died on Saturday,

Buried on Sunday,

This is the end

of Solomon Grundy.

fasten
 see join, shut

fear
 see fright

feeble
 see weak

feel

feel *(verb)*

If you come into contact with something, or get an impression of something, you **feel** it: *This cloth **feels** like silk; it's so smooth.*

experience   You'll **experience** a sense of achievement when you have learned to swim.

handle   **Handle** the china with great care.

sense   Sue **sensed** that something was wrong.

suffer   If you have toothache, you will **suffer** some pain.

touch   If I reach up high enough, I can **touch** the ceiling.

see also touch

fetch
see get

few
see opposite
of many

fight

fight *(verb)*

When you **fight**, you try to hurt somebody, or you make an effort to do something: *I had to **fight** to get people to listen to my story.*

battle   The wrestlers **battled** for the world championship.

combat   Judge Smith will always **combat** every form of injustice.

oppose   The local people **opposed** the plan for a new service station.

quarrel   I'm sorry Naomi and I **quarrelled**; she's my best friend.

struggle   Jack **struggled** to knot his tie.

Opposite words: **agree** *see* say

reconcile   My two brothers had argued for years, but are now **reconciled**.

filled
  see full

filthy
  see dirty

find →

fine
  see good, thin

finger
  see touch

finish
  see end

firm
  see fast, hard, strong, sure

fit
  see good

fix
  see opposite of break

flat
  see smooth

flee
  see escape

flimsy
  see light, weak

find *(verb)*

If you unearth something, or come across it unexpectedly, you **find** it: *Let's go to the beach and see if we can **find** some seashells.*

discover   We **discovered** a mistake in the book.

locate   Can you **locate** your home town on the map?

trace   The police were unable to **trace** the missing painting.

work out   Can you **work out** the answer?

Opposite word

lose   I would hate to **lose** my watch.

see also opposite of hide

float
  see rise

flow
  see run

fluffy
  see soft

flutter
  see shake

foe
  see opposite of friend

force
  see push

forgetful
  see opposite of careful

form
see make

forsake
see leave *and*
opposite of keep

foul
see dirty

fracture
see break

fragment
see piece

frail
see weak

frank
see plain

fraudulent
see opposite
of fair

freezing
see cold

frequent
see many

friend

friend *(noun)*

Anyone who is pleasant, and whom you know well and like, can be called a **friend**: *Friends* like doing things together.

acquaintance   I don't know him well; he's more of an **acquaintance** than a friend.

companion   She was my **companion** at school and when we worked in an office.

comrade   Andy was my **comrade** when we were in the army together.

pal   Meet Jeff, an old **pal** of mine.

Opposite words

enemy   Moriarty was a deadly **enemy** of Sherlock Holmes.

foe   Who goes there? Friend or **foe**?

friendless
  see lonely

friendly
  see good *and*
  opposite of angry

fright

fright *(noun)*

When you feel afraid or fearful, you are experiencing **fright**: *I had a terrible **fright** when I thought I saw a ghost.*

alarm   Shouts of **alarm** arose as the soldiers entered the town.

dismay   We looked with **dismay** at the wreckage left by the storm.

fear   The antelope's eyes were wide with **fear** as the lion sprang.

panic   The flood waters swirled into the town, spreading **panic**.

terror   The greatest **terror** of the jungle is fire.

frightened
see afraid

fry
see cook

full

full *(adjective)*

If something is **full**, there is no space for anything more: *We couldn't get seats for the theatre because it was* **full**.

complete   Jennifer has a **complete** set of stamps for the Olympic Games.

entire   I received a class prize in front of the **entire** school.

filled   All the **filled** bags were loaded on to the truck.

packed   The attic is **packed** with junk.

Other words bulging, crammed, jammed, overflowing

Opposite words *see* empty

funny

funny

furious
see angry

funny *(adjective)*

Anything that makes you laugh or that is unusual or surprising, can be called **funny**: *There were many funny people in the movies, but the best was Charlie Chaplin.*

amusing The children like Clare; she's such an **amusing** talker.

comical With her battered hat and false nose, she was a **comical** clown.

humorous The audience roared with laughter at the comedian's **humorous** stories.

odd Dad's face wore an **odd** expression as he opened the door.

strange Martha's voice sounded **strange**, and she looked frightened.

see also odd

Other words hilarious, peculiar, ridiculous, witty

Opposite words

serious I am sorry to say I have some **serious** news.

see also sad

50

G

gain
  see get

gather
  see pick

gaze
  see look

generous
  see kind *and*
  opposite of mean

gentle
  see kind,
  quiet, soft

get

get up
  see rise

get *(verb)*

If you take, buy, or are given something, you **get** it: *I suggest you **get** a new pair of socks; those won't last much longer.*

become	Do you really **become** wiser as you get older?
bring	Spring often **brings** fine weather.
collect	Will you **collect** the dry-cleaning?
earn	My brother has a new job, and he **earns** twice what I **earn**!
fetch	My dog likes to **fetch** sticks.
gain	We **gained** a lot of knowledge from our trip to the museum.
obtain	We **obtain** a lot of news from radio.
receive	We **received** a great welcome.
win	Sarah Bernhardt **won** the applause of audiences everywhere.

giggle
see laugh

give

give *(verb)*

To **give** is to hand something over to someone for them to keep: *Please **give** me something to eat.*

bestow The college **bestowed** the trophy on its football team.

donate In her will, Dr Brown **donated** a large sum of money to her old hospital.

grant I was **granted** leave so that I could make a trip to Africa.

offer Can I **offer** you a lift home?

present We would like to **present** you with this gift on your retirement.

provide Peter **provided** the food for the camping trip.

supply We can **supply** everything you need for building your house.

Opposite words

deny I cannot **deny** you the chance to visit Alaska.

retain Did you **retain** part of the ticket?

withhold Tell the whole story and don't **withhold** anything.

glad
 see happy

glide
 see slide

gloomy
 see dull, sad

go

go *(verb)*

You **go** if you advance from one place to another: *I usually go to school by bus, but I come home by car.*

continue   The road **continues** for miles.

depart   We **depart** tomorrow for Israel.

leave   What time does the plane **leave**?

move   We **moved** back to Scotland.

pass   Many years **passed** before we met again.

proceed   After lunch we **proceeded** on our way.

travel   We **travelled** through the night and arrived home at 5 a.m.

vanish   After we set off for Peru, Mary **vanished**. I never saw her again.

see also leave, turn, walk

Opposite words

stop   We **stopped** at a hotel by the sea.

see also come

good

gorge
  see eat

grab
  see catch

gradual
  *see opposite
  of* fast

grant
  see give

grasp
  see hold, take

great
  see big,
  important

grill
  see cook

grimy
  see dirty

grin
  see laugh

grip
  see hold

grope
  see touch

good (*adjective*)

Anything that is **good** is of high quality or the best of its kind: *Alison and John are **good** pupils and will do well at college.*

admirable	Her behaviour is **admirable**.
excellent	He was a good violinist and an **excellent** pianist.
fine	Here is a first-class shop which has **fine** jewellery.
fit	A marvellous meal **fit** for a king!
friendly	We are lucky in having **friendly**, thoughtful neighbours.
kind	She is a helpful, **kind** old lady.
pleasant	Brittany is **pleasant** in spring.
right	It's important that children are taught **right** from wrong.
sound	This radio is old, but **sound**.
suitable	Is Tuesday **suitable** or would Thursday be more convenient?

see also kind, right

Other words expert, fantastic, splendid, superb, terrific

Opposite words *see* bad

grow *(verb)*

If something **grows**, it becomes bigger, larger, longer, or taller: *My fingernails have **grown** quite long; I'll have to cut them.*

become   Tom **became** tired of his old bicycle and asked for a new one.

develop   Her small workshop **developed** into a factory.

enlarge   This part of the map shows an **enlarged** plan of the town centre.

extend   My telescope **extends** to 9 inches.

increase   The number of children in the mosque school **increased** by 50.

Opposite words

decrease   The number of people wearing hats has **decreased**.

see also opposite of rise

H

hamper
see opposite of help

handle
see feel, touch

handsome
see beautiful

happen
see come

happy

happy *(adjective)*

If you are pleased and in a good mood, you can be called **happy**: *We went to Ben's bar mitzvah, and everyone was **happy**.*

cheerful My brother is always **cheerful**; he's such a joker.

contented I've finished all my work for today, and I'm **contented**.

delighted Bill and Sue were **delighted** with their beautiful wedding presents.

glad I'm **glad** you like my new dog.

joyful Christmas is a **joyful** occasion, and Thanksgiving is a merry time too.

Other words carefree, jolly, merry, satisfied

see also opposite of sad

hard

hardy
see strong

harm
see hurt

harsh
see hard *and*
opposite of kind

hasten
see hurry

haul
see pull

heal
see opposite
of hurt

heavy
see big *and*
opposite of thin

hard *(adjective)*

Anything that is not soft, or is solid, is called **hard**: *We spread the cement over the path and waited for it to get* **hard**. **Hard** can also mean 'not easy to do'.

awful   Somalia's civil war has made life **awful** for many.

complicated I can't work out this problem; it's much too **complicated**.

dense   Mahogany is a **dense** wood.

difficult   We must save money, as there are **difficult** times ahead.

firm   The chairs were well-made; **firm** and strong.

harsh   The judge is always **harsh** to criminals, and shows no mercy.

stern   My granny is **stern**, but fair.

stiff   The shoebox is made of **stiff** cardboard.

tough   I can't eat this nougat; it's too **tough** and chewy!

Opposite words

mild   I always use a **mild** shampoo.

see also soft

help

helpful
  see kind

helpless
  see weak

help *(verb)*

If you do something to make life easier for someone else, you **help** them: *I like to **help** my parents around the house.*

aid   Harry **aided** Beth to look for her hearing aid.

assist   Carole **assisted** Sióbhan with her homework.

improve These pills will **improve** your digestion.

serve   Jo **served** the company for 9 years.

support Most people **supported** Dr. Stein in her search for a cure.

Opposite words

hamper   Your chatter is **hampering** my concentration.

hinder   I would have arrived earlier, but was **hindered** by the potholes in the road.

hide

hide *(verb)*

When you **hide** something, you put it out of sight, where others cannot see it: *If you are quiet and **hide** in the bushes, you will see a lot of wildlife.*

bury   Bonzo **buried** his bone in the garden.

conceal   The magician **concealed** the cards up her sleeve.

cover   At night the parrot cage is **covered** with a cloth.

disguise   Vanessa **disguised** herself as a ghost at Hallowe'en.

mask   The Moon **masks** the Sun during a solar eclipse.

Opposite words *see* find, show

hike
  see walk

hinder
  see opposite of help

hit

hit *(verb)*

If you bang or bash something hard, you can also say that you **hit** it: *The player **hit** the ball against the wall.*

beat   Beat the rug to get out the dust.

bump   In the dark Dylan **bumped** into a lamppost.

knock   Somebody **knocked** on the door at midnight.

smack   Sam **smacked** the naughty puppy.

strike   Jill **struck** the nail with a hammer.

tap   Someone **tapped** me on the arm.

thump Liz **thumped** the table in a rage.

Other words bang, bash, batter, collide, hammer, flog, whip

hold

hold *(verb)*

You **hold** something if you have it firmly in your hand: *Hold onto that rope! Help is on the way!*

clutch   My little brother **clutched** my hand as we crossed the road.

contain   This box **contains** pizza for lunch.

grasp   Peggy **grasped** the horse's reins as it galloped out of control.

grip   Gwyneth **gripped** the spade and began to dig.

possess   The family has **possessed** this plantation for centuries.

see also keep

Same sound

holed   The boat was **holed** and water gushed in.

Opposite word

release   Sam **released** the bird from its cage.

Houses

Where do you live?

An adobe house
in South America

An African village
house

An Alpine chalet

A log cabin in the
forests of Canada

A caravan

A Native
American tepee

A house with a flat roof
in North America

A house on stilts in Borneo

Double words
Fill in the missing word in the centre of each line, remembering that
the clues each side refer to it.

hut _ _ _ _ spill   garden _ _ _ _ three feet

apartment _ _ _ _ level   road _ _ _ method

62

A bungalow by the seaside

Odd one out

The White House

Sydney Harbour Bridge

The Eiffel Tower

The Tower of Babel

Few people now
live in castles.

A house

A houseboat

Skyscrapers save space
in big cities.

Put in the missing letters to make a word that is the name of a part of a house:

w _ n _ ow   do _ r   c _ imn _ y   roo _   f _ o _ r

wa _ l   ce _ l _ ng   st _ i _ s

honest
  see right

hot
  see opposite
  of cold

huge
  see big

humorous
  see funny

hurry

hurry *(verb)*

If you **hurry**, you move or do something quickly, often because there's not enough time: *Please **hurry** with my breakfast, I have to catch a train.*

dash The naughty dog **dashed** after the frightened cat.

hasten Husain **hastened** his step to keep up with the others.

race Jo **raced** to the phone as it rang.

run Look at the ants! They **run** in all directions.

rush The ambulance **rushed** to the hospital.

speed Howard was stopped for **speeding** down the motorway.

see also run

Opposite words

dawdle Stop **dawdling** and catch up!

delay All flights are **delayed** because of ice and snow.

linger After the reception, the guests **lingered** in the lobby.

hurt

hush
*see opposite
of* noise

hushed
see quiet

hurt *(verb)*

When you **hurt** somebody you cause them pain or distress: *What you said was very cruel, and it **hurt** me a lot.*

ache   The din makes my ears **ache**.

damage   The town was **damaged** by the earthquake.

harm   Did the wolf **harm** the hens?

injure   Rachel **injured** her back in a riding accident.

upset   Watching the sad film **upset** Henry.

wound   Fred was **wounded** in battle and has a bad limp.

Opposite words

console   After her kitten died, nothing could **console** our poor cat.

heal   This cream will **heal** anything!

soothe   What a **soothing** voice you have.

I

illustration
see picture

important

improper
*see opposite
of* right

improve
see help

impure
see dirty

incorrect
see wrong

increase
see grow, rise

indicate
see mean, show

important *(adjective)*

Something that is serious and matters a great deal is said to be **important**: *This book gives a list of the most **important** dates in history.*

famous   Greta Garbo was a **famous** Hollywood film star.

great   La Scala in Milan is one of the world's **great** opera houses.

main   The **main** cities of Zimbabwe are Harare and Bulawayo.

necessary   Water is **necessary** for all life.

Opposite words

minor   **Minor** and miner sound the same but have a **minor** spelling difference.

petty   **Petty** details are unimportant.

indignant
see angry

injure
see hurt

insist
see say

inspect
see see

intelligent
see clever

intend
see mean

interesting

introduce
see start

invent
see make

invite
see ask

irate
see angry

interesting *(adjective)*

Something that holds your attention, or that you want to know more about, is **interesting**: *This magazine has an **interesting** article on the Ainu people of Japan.*

entertaining   She has such **entertaining** stories about the old days.

fascinating   Sharon finds ancient Egyptian history **fascinating**.

pleasing   What a **pleasing** view of the old church.

Opposite words *see* dull

J

job
see work

join

jostle
see push

joyful
see happy

just
see fair, right

join *(verb)*

When you **join** things, you put them together: *To splice, you **join** two short pieces of rope together to make one long one.* **Join** can also mean 'to become a member of': *We **joined** the football club.*

connect　The Channel Tunnel **connects** France and Britain.

fasten　Judy **fastened** the papers together with a stapler.

link　The trailer is **linked** to the tractor.

unite　We all **united** to fight the enemy.

Opposite words

disconnect　When we moved house, the telephone was **disconnected**.

separate　Sudan is **separated** from Saudi Arabia by the Red Sea.

keep *(verb)*

If you have something, and do not give it to someone else, you **keep** it: *I shall always **keep** this ring; it will remind me of you.*

continue   I'm too tired to **continue** playing.

hold   Catherine **held** the coins.

observe   The first of May is **observed** in many countries as a holiday.

retain   I **retain** a vivid memory of what he looked like.

save   **Save** this coupon for a free gift!

see also hold

Opposite words

discard   I **discarded** my winter clothes.

forsake   My father loved cigars, but decided to **forsake** smoking altogether.

throw away Please **throw away** that rubbish!

kind

kind *(adjective)*

Kind people are always ready to help others: *Anthony is **kind** to all animals.*

generous   Judy is **generous** and always shares her sweets.

gentle   Jim gave his friend a **gentle** hug.

helpful   You've been very **helpful** showing me the way.

tender   I gave my puppy a **tender** look.

see also good

Opposite words

harsh   The angry shopkeeper spoke to us in **harsh** words.

severe   There are **severe** laws in Peru.

see also hard

kindle
  see light

knock
  see hit

know

know *(verb)*

If you **know** something, it is in your mind and you are aware of what it is about: *She always **knows** all the answers.*

recall   I **recall** his face very well, but I've forgotten his name!

recognize   I didn't **recognize** you in those dark glasses.

understand   I lived in Japan for a year, so I **understand** Japanese.

see also think

Same sound

no   (*adjective*) There's **no** knowing what will happen.

L

labour
see work

lamp
see light

large
see big *and*
opposite of small

laugh

laugh *(verb)*

When you hear, see, or think of something funny, you **laugh**: *The Marx Brothers made nearly everyone **laugh**.*

chuckle Laura **chuckled** to herself as she read the funny book.

giggle He told a lot of silly jokes, but they made us all **giggle**.

grin Louise **grinned** when Jim gave her a present.

smile **Smile** and the whole world **smiles** with you.

snigger Some people **sniggered** when Joe slipped on the banana skin, but I didn't think it was funny.

Opposite words

cry The sad story made Chris **cry**.

launch
   see send

lay
   see put

lean
   see thin

leave

leave *(verb)*

If you go away from somewhere, you **leave**: *I have to **leave** Calcutta tomorrow, as I'm due in Tokyo on Monday.*

abandon We've struck an iceberg! **Abandon** ship!

depart   We're going to Jamaica and we **depart** early next month.

desert   Paul Gauguin, the artist, **deserted** his family and went to the South Seas.

forsake   Joe has **forsaken** his old carefree life and become a Buddhist monk.

quit   After 20 years, he **quit** the circus and settled down.

see also go

Opposite words

arrive   My family **arrived** to meet me when I stepped off the plane.

see also come

Land names

Which of these features can you see on this page?
continent isthmus plateau / ocean sea bay gulf / beach coast
sand shore / cliff precipice / valley canyon fjord gorge /
river wadi stream brook burn delta estuary /
hill mountain slope range elevation mount /
desert tundra wasteland dune / forest wood
copse spinney jungle / savanna steppes
pampas plain grasslands prairie /
coral reef / bush outback / oasis
watering hole / island isle
peninsula / marsh bog
swamp quicksand /
volcano geyser

Hidden rivers
Find the rivers hidden in these sentences.
1. Soon I leave this country for a boat tour of the world.
2. After the first thud, sonic boom waves were blamed for the damage.
3. When meat is used with spaghetti, gristle, fat, and bone must be removed.

What animal lives where?
camel kangaroo eagle cattle squirrel dolphin

Same sound

beach / *beech*
shore / *sure*
isle / *I'll, aisle*

steppes / *steps*
wood / *would*
sea / *see*

Say it either way
Niagara, O roar again
Able was I, ere I saw Elba

level
  see smooth

light

light *(adjective)*

If something is not heavy and has very little weight, we say that it's **light**: *I'll carry your bag for you; it's as **light** as a feather.* **Light** is also the power that makes it possible for us to see things: *The Sun gives off bright **light**.*

airy   *Full of fresh air and breezes*: What a bright and **airy** room!

buoyant   The rubber dinghy was **buoyant**, floating about on the waves.

flimsy   The hut was so **flimsy** that the wind blew it down one night.

pale   Her dress was pink, or perhaps you could call it **pale** red.

kindle   *(verb) To light a fire*: **Kindle** those sticks and we'll soon have a fire.

lamp   *(noun)* We like to keep the **lamp** lit in the porch.

see also fair

Other words *(verb)* burn, flare, ignite, illuminate, gleam, glitter, sparkle

like

like *(verb)*

If you think a person or thing is pleasant, then you **like** it: *I **like** most sweet things, but my favourite is chocolate.*

admire   I **admire** doctors and nurses because they help sick people.

love   I **love** being beside the sea.

prefer   I play many sports, but I **prefer** basketball.

see also love

linger
*see opposite
of* hurry

link
see join

little
see small *and
opposite of* big

load
see put

locate
see find

lock
see shut

lonely

lonesome
see lonely

lonely *(adjective)*

If you are on your own, without friends, you can say that you are **lonely**: *Big cities are full of people, but you can feel* **lonely** *there.*

alone   Robinson Crusoe lived all **alone** on a desert island.

friendless   I was quite **friendless** when I arrived in the big city.

lonesome   Abdul felt **lonesome** and home-sick in that distant country.

solitary   As I crossed the remote moor, I saw just one **solitary** house.

look

look *(verb)*

When you use your eyes to see something, you **look**: *Look at the sunset; it's beautiful.*

gaze Sarah **gazed** at the butterflies.

notice Have you ever **noticed** Neil's knobbly knees?

regard The professor **regarded** her students through thick-lensed spectacles.

see He shaded his eyes to **see** across the rippling water.

seem Larry **seems** to be younger than he really is.

stare I **stared** with horror as the scorpion crawled nearer.

watch **Watch** out for a number 22 bus.

see also see

lose
see opposite of find

loud

loud *(adjective)*

If something is easy to hear or makes a lot of noise, we say that it's **loud**: *Turn down the radio, please; it's too **loud**.*

boisterous   The quiet town was invaded by **boisterous** football fans.

noisy   It was a **noisy** meeting, and we had to shout to be heard.

raucous   That harsh, **raucous** noise is Ted practising on his trumpet.

showy   He wore a **showy**, large-patterned check suit.

shrill   The **shrill** sound of a whistle is earsplitting.

see also noisy

Opposite words *see* quiet, soft

love

lovely
  see beautiful

love *(verb)*

If you have a strong liking for, or a great attraction to, something or someone, you can use the word **love**: *I love my family with all my heart.*

adore   Guy **adores** his grandad.

like   I **like** most kinds of music.

worship   Warren **worships** his uncle.

affection *(noun)* I have a great **affection** for all animals.

esteem   *(noun)* The author of that book is held in high **esteem** by her readers.

see also like

M

mad
  see angry

main
  see important

make

make *(verb)*

If we **make** something, we put other things together, or create it: *Jack just **made** a crane with his construction set.* **Make** can also mean 'to cause something to happen'.

build   I'm **building** a tree house.

compel   It rained so much, we were **compelled** to stay at home.

construct   Ann learned how to **construct** a model car.

earn   How much do you **earn** in your new job?

form   We **formed** a society for those interested in painting.

invent   Printing was **invented** by the Chinese.

manufacture   The Koreans **manufacture** cars and bikes.

mould   The potter **moulded** a pot out of the clay.

prepare   Dad **prepared** dinner for us.

Opposite words

destroy   The storm **destroyed** the boat.

undo   Can you **undo** the knot?

manufacture
see make

many

many *(adjective)*

If you have a large number of something, then you could say you have **many**: *Were there **many** children in class today?*

frequent   Mark makes **frequent** visits to our house. He comes several times a week.

numerous   We advertised in the local paper and had **numerous** replies.

Opposite words

few   **Few** people like snakes.

rare   Butterflies are **rare** in Greenland.

march
  see walk

mask
  see hide

mean

mediocre
  see fair

mend
  see opposite
  of break

mean *(verb)*

When we **mean** something, we show it, are serious about it, or explain it: *Dictionaries are books that tell us what words **mean**.* **Mean** as an *adjective* can describe someone who is not generous.

indicate   The hands on a clock **indicate** what time it is.

intend   I **intend** to go to the zoo tomorrow.

nasty   (*adjective*) Meg said **nasty**, spiteful things about her boss.

stingy   (*adjective*) Scrooge had always been miserly and **stingy**, but later was kind to Tiny Tim.

unkind   (*adjective*) It was selfish and **unkind** of you not to ask Clara to your party.

Opposite word

generous   Ruth is very successful but she's always **generous** to her staff.

mess

mild
see quiet *and opposite of* hard

mingle
see mix

minor
see opposite of important

minute
see small

miserable
see sad

mistaken
see wrong

misty
see opposite of clear

mess *(noun)*

If someone or something is in a **mess**, they are dirty, untidy, or mixed up: *This room is a complete **mess**.*

clutter   In the wardrobe there was a **clutter** of old clothes.

difficulty   She got into **difficulty** and had to be rescued.

muddle   My desk is in a real **muddle**; I'll have to tidy it.

Music

Instruments around the world

In every part of the world people play musical instruments. Some instruments have remained unchanged for hundreds of years; others, like the steel drum of the West Indies, made from oil drums, are recent.

Steel drums from the West Indies

Bagpipes
from Scotland

Banjo from the USA

Panpipes from
South America

Musical memory
Mnemonics (pronounced nem on ics), or memory aids, are named after the Greek goddess of memory, Mnemosyne. Here are two musical examples: The lines and spaces of the treble stave in written music are: E F G A B C D E F; those of the bass stave are G A B C D E F G A. These silly sentences may help you remember them: **E**very **F**ine **G**irl **A**nd **B**oy **C**an **D**efinitely **E**at **F**ish and **G**ood **A**nd **B**ad **C**ats **D**on't **E**ver **F**ind **G**reen **A**nts.

Sound the same
band	banned
reed (*of a pipe*)	read
keys (*of a piano*)	quays (*in a port*)
cymbals (*you hit*)	symbols (*signs*)

Sound different
bass	bass
(*deep male voice*)	(*a kind of fish*)
bow	bow
(*of a violin*)	(*a greeting*)

Songs with different tunes
song anthem carol hymn lullaby pop song nursery rhyme

Groups of Instruments

In an orchestra there are four main groups of instruments:
string instruments that are plucked or played with a bow.
woodwind instruments made of wood or metal. The player blows into or across the mouthpiece.
brass instruments made of metal.
percussion instruments that are hit or shaken.

See if you can place these instruments in their right group:

harp violin clarinet xylophone cello guitar tambourine double bass oboe gong trumpet trombone

Didgeridoo from Australia

Koto from Japan

Sitar from India

Balalaika from Russia

Gamelan orchestra from Indonesia

mix

modern
see opposite of old

modify
see change

moist
see wet

moisten
see wet

mould
see make

move
see go

muddle
see mess

mix *(verb)*

If you put things together, or shake them, you **mix** them: *To make the cake, put all the ingredients together and **mix** them in a bowl.*

blend   You **blend** flour and water to make paste.

combine   The orchestra and choir were **combined** for a special performance.

mingle   It was a great party; everyone **mingled** quite happily.

shuffle   Please **shuffle** the cards.

stir   Sue **stirred** sugar into her tea.

N

name
  see call

narrow
  see thin

nasty
  see bad, mean,
  and opposite
  of nice

naughty
  see bad

nearly
  see about

necessary
  see important

nervous
  see afraid

new
  see opposite
  of old

nibble
  see eat

nice

nice *(adjective)*

Someone or something you like or find attractive, is **nice**: *I would like a **nice** cool drink. She's a very **nice** girl. Isn't it **nice** here?*

comfortable The kittens are sleeping on a cosy, **comfortable** cushion.

delicious This plum is **delicious**!

enjoyable Summer camp was **enjoyable**.

pleasant We spent a **pleasant** week in a charming Swiss village.

smart What **smart**, stylish, and elegant clothes they wear!

thoughtful It was **thoughtful** and kind of you to look after my dog.

see also beautiful, fair, good, interesting, kind

Opposite words

nasty That's a **nasty** cut.

rude It's **rude** to say, "Shut up".

noise

noisy
see loud *and*
opposite of quiet

normal
see opposite
of odd

notice
see look, see

numerous
see many

noise *(noun)*

We sometimes speak of **noise** when what we hear is loud and unpleasant: *We live near the airport, and the aircraft **noise** is terrible.*

clamour   A hundred people all talking at once makes quite a **clamour**.

din   There was such a **din**, I couldn't hear myself talk.

racket   This morning the crows were making an awful **racket**.

row   The animals at feeding time make quite a **row**.

sound   **Sounds** can be loud and deafening, or soft and soothing.

Opposite words

hush   There was a **hush** when the teacher appeared.

silence   I need complete **silence** to be able to concentrate.

O

observe
see keep, see

obtain
see get

obvious
see clear, plain

occupied
see opposite
of empty

occur
see come

odd

odd *(adjective)*

If something is **odd**, it is not ordinary or usual: *The Horny Goloch sounds like a very **odd** animal.* Or, it can mean 'left over', 'not even', or 'not alike': *I always seem to have several **odd** socks. Two is an even number, three is an **odd** one.*

peculiar　It's **peculiar** for a lobster to blow its nose.

quaint　There are many **quaint** villages here.

strange　I had a **strange** dream about a weird worm.

unusual　It's **unusual** to see an octopus knitting.

see also funny

Opposite words

even　Four is an **even** number.

normal　It's **normal** to want to play out on a sunny day.

usual　I took the **usual** way home.

offer
see give

old

open
see start

operate
see work

oppose
see fight

ordinary
see plain

old *(adjective)*

Anyone who has lived for a long time, or anything that has existed for a long time, is **old**: *This armchair is very **old**; it was my great-grandmother's.*

aged Professor Mills looks after her **aged** mother.

ancient Excavations in Benin showed relics of the **ancient** civilization.

antique My uncle is interested in really old things, and collects **antique** silver.

worn You should buy a new jacket; that one is shabby and **worn**.

Opposite words

modern The computer is a **modern** invention.

new **New** leaves come out in spring.

recent What's the most **recent** news?

young All **young** animals are cute.

P

packed
see full
and opposite
of empty

painting
see picture

pal
see friend

pale
see light

panic
see fright

parched
see dry
and opposite
of wet

part
see piece

pass
see go

peaceful
see calm, quiet

peculiar
see odd

peer
see see

performance
see show

petty
see opposite
of important

photograph
see picture

pick *(verb)*

If you **pick** something, you remove it or you decide to take it from a selection offered to you: *Pick one of these cards.*

choose Brenda **chose** the biggest piece of cake.

gather Let's go out and **gather** some logs for our winter fires.

pluck Jeff **plucked** an apple from the tree and began to munch it.

select Jane **selected** some tomatoes and walked to the check-out counter.

pick

picture

picture *(noun)*

If you put an image on paper or other surface, you make a **picture**: *I like books with plenty of pictures in them.*

drawing   A **drawing** is a picture in pen or pencil.

illustration   This book has colour **illustrations**.

painting   The Mona Lisa is the most famous **painting** in the world.

photograph   Kay used her new camera to take a **photograph** of the giraffe.

portrait   This is a **portrait** of my great-aunt.

sketch   Mustapha did a quick **sketch** of the new mosque.

piece

place
see put

placid
see calm

piece *(noun)*

A small section of something is called a **piece**: *That chocolate cake looks delicious. May I have a **piece**?*

bit   Look at my vase! It's broken into tiny **bits**.

fragment   The window smashed, and **fragments** of glass flew every-where.

part   This **part** of the building is used as a library.

portion   After the duke died, a large **portion** of his lands became a public garden.

Other words   chip, chunk, portion, slice, splinter

Same sound

peace   My brother needs **peace** and quiet to study.

plain

pleasant
see good, nice

pleased
see opposite of angry

pleasing
see interesting

pliable
see soft

pluck
see pick

plunge
see push

poke
see push

polished
see smooth

polluted
see dirty

portion
see piece

portrait
see picture

plain (adjective)

Something that is not complicated, and has no decoration, is called **plain**: *Jill made good furniture; it was **plain** but strong.* **Plain** can also mean 'not pretty'.

frank	I'll give you a **frank** reply: I didn't like the play at all.
obvious	The answer to this easy question is **obvious**.
ordinary	Andy's just an **ordinary** fellow; he doesn't try to be clever.
simple	This is an old-fashioned village, and we all live **simple** lives.

see also clear

Same sound

plane	(*noun*) Pete took the plane to Pittsburgh.

Opposite word

complicated	I can't do algebra; it's much too **complicated** for me.

possess
see hold

post
see send

powerful
 see strong

prefer
 see like

prepare
 see make

present
 see give

press
 see push

pretty
 see beautiful

proceed
 see go

pronounce
 see say

propel
 see push

proper
 see right *and*
 opposite of wrong

provide
 see give

prune
 see cut

pull ➡

pull *(verb)*

If you get hold of something and make it come towards you, you **pull** it: *In the old days, steam locomotives were used to **pull** trains.*

drag   Debra helped Isabel **drag** the desk across the room.

draw   Black horses are used to **draw** the queen's coach.

haul   We must all **haul** on this rope to bring up the sail.

stretch   I **stretched** the rope across the yard to make a clothesline.

tug   He **tugged** hard at the knob, but he couldn't open the door.

Other words
heave, tow

Opposite words
see push

Plants

All flowering plants have the same four main parts: roots, stems, leaves, flowers. Most make new plants by growing seeds. Non-flowering plants can't make seeds. They make new plants with spores (tiny cells). Mosses and bracken are non-flowering plants, and so is seaweed.

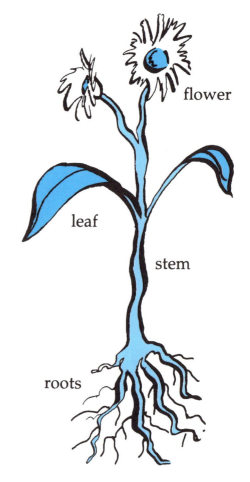

The parts of a plant

Fruit, flower, vegetable, or tree?
Group these plants and put them in the correct alphabetical order:

pear	bean
elm	iris
apple	pea
grape	daffodil
lettuce	celery
beech	pineapple
onion	daisy
avocado	cauliflower
nut	lemon
lily	oak
carrot	cassava
tulip	nasturtium

A weather forecasting rhyme
Oak before ash
You're in for a splash.
Ash before oak
You're in for a soak.

The Language of Flowers

Some flowers have traditional meanings if you give them as a present. Here are some examples:

apple blossom *you are preferred*
balm *sympathy*
bluebell *true and tender*
iris *have faith in me*
ivy *I cling*
olive *peace*
pansy *thoughts*

poppy *forgetfulness*
red rose *love*
rosemary *remembrance*
sunflower *adoration*
sweet william *pleasant dreams*
white clover *think of me*

Try writing someone a letter, drawing a picture of a flower instead of using the word.

Some plant homonyms

bough / *bow*
beach / *beech*
berry / *bury*
cereal / *serial*
currant / *current*
fir / *fur*
flour / *flower*
lichen / *liken*
plum / *plumb*
rye / *wry*
time / *thyme*
weed / *we'd*
wood / *would*

Roots

Can you complete these words without using a dictionary?

geran _ _ _   tu _ _ _   da _ _ _

dandel _ _ _   chrysan _ _ _ _ _ _

sunflo _ _ _   marigo _ _   wallf _ _ _ _ _

puny
  see small, weak

pure
  see clear

push

push *(verb)*

If you apply force to something to make it move away from you, you **push** it: *Tim's car broke down on a hill, so we all had to get out and push it.*

force Angela had lost her key, so she had to **force** her suitcase open.

jostle When the big parade went by, we were **jostled** by the crowds.

plunge We **plunged** through the driving snow.

poke Our ball got lodged in a drain-pipe, but I **poked** it out.

press **Press** the button to ring the doorbell.

propel I felt a strong push in the back, which **propelled** me forward.

thrust Mark **thrust** several coins into his pocket.

Other words bump, cram, nudge, shove

Opposite words *see* pull

put →

put *(verb)*

When you move something into position, you **put** it there: *All our warm clothes were **put** away for the summer.*

deposit   I **deposited** my hat and coat in the cloakroom.

lay   **Lay** all your cards on the table.

load   Larry **loaded** the washing machine.

place   She **placed** her foot firmly on the first step of the ladder.

set   Jill **set** a heavy package on the table.

stand   **Stand** that clock on the shelf.

stick   Our dog always **sticks** its head out of the car window.

Opposite words

remove   I must ask you to **remove** all this clutter immediately.

withdraw   We went to the bank and **withdrew** enough money to pay for my bicycle.

Q

quaint
see odd

quarrel
see fight

query
see ask

quick
see fast

quiet

quit
see leave

quiver
see shake

quiet *(adjective)*

When there is no sound or noise, it is **quiet**: *The house was so **quiet** that it seemed rather spooky.*

calm   The storm had quietened down, and now the sea was **calm**.

gentle   Alison has a **gentle**, soothing voice.

mild   Johnny is a **mild**, sweet person.

peaceful   After the war, we all looked forward to **peaceful** times.

silent   We stood **silent**, looking at the badgers.

tranquil   I went for a walk at dawn, a very **tranquil** time.

see also calm, soft, *and opposite of* loud

Other words   hushed, shy, timid

Opposite words

disturbing   The constant banging of the door is very **disturbing**.

noisy   My sleep was broken by the **noisy** seagulls.

R

race
see hurry, run

racket
see noise

rainy
see wet

rapid
see fast

rare
*see opposite
of* many

rash
*see opposite
of* careful

raucous
see loud

reasonable
see fair

recall
see know

receive
see get *and
opposite of* send

recent
*see opposite
of* old

recite
see say

recognize
see know

reconcile
*see opposite
of* fight

regard
see look

reject
*see opposite
of* take

relax
see rest

release
see opposite of
catch, hold

remainder
see rest

remark
see say

remove
*see opposite
of* put

repair
*see opposite
of* break

reply
see say

repose
see rest

request
see ask

rest *(verb)*

If you are working hard, you might stop to **rest**: *We've been walking for hours; we ought to rest*. **Rest** as a *noun* also means 'what is left over': *I've eaten most of the cherries, but you can have the **rest**.*

relax   Emma has been exercising very hard. Now she must **relax**.

repose   A necklace **reposed** on the cushion.

sleep   I lay on the sofa and **slept**.

remainder   *(noun)* Some children went home for lunch, but the **remainder** ate sandwiches at school.

Other words *(noun)* remnant, residue, *(verb)* slumber, snooze

retain
see keep *and opposite of* change, give

reveal
see show

right

right *(adjective)*

When we speak of the **right** thing, we mean the correct, true, or the best thing: *Is this the right road for Jane's house?* **Right** is also the opposite of left.

correct   Do you have the **correct** time?

good   If you need a wristwatch, I'll buy you a **good** one.

honest   I'll be **honest** with you; I don't like this food.

just   It was only **just** that Tina should get the job rather than Bill.

proper   Before we can do the repairs, we must have the **proper** tools.

suitable   Is this scarf **suitable** for summer?

upright   Everyone trusts the rabbi, for he is an **upright**, good person.

see also fair, good

Opposite words

false   I'm sorry, but this ring is **false**. It's not gold at all.

improper   Those boots are quite **improper** for ballet dancing!

see also wrong

rise

rise *(verb)*

If you stand up, or go upwards, you **rise**:
*Everyone **rises** when the judge enters the court.
The balloon began to **rise** slowly.*

ascend   We **ascended** the long, winding
                    stairway to the attic.

float   Jenny watched the bubbles **float**
                    away.

get up   Hurry! It's time to **get up**!

increase   Our prices will **increase** from
                    tomorrow.

soar   The eagle **soared** into the sky.

Other words climb, stand up, take off

Opposite words

decline   She's not well; her health has
                    declined over the last year.

decrease   Our speed **decreased** to a snail's
                    pace.

descend   The lift **descended** to the
                    basement.

sink   The Sun **sinks** in the west.

roast
see cook

robust
see strong

rotten
see bad

rough

rough (*adjective*)

If something is not smooth, or is wild and noisy, we say it is **rough**: *We can't drive our car over the bumpy, **rough** ground.*

boisterous They don't mean any harm; they're just rowdy, **boisterous** children.

coarse The prisoners wore uniforms made of **coarse** material.

crude The first tools were quite **crude**.

rugged The mountain road is **rugged**.

stormy The sea was **stormy** and everyone felt sea-sick.

uneven It's an old house, with **uneven** floors and ceilings.

Same sound

ruff (*noun*) The poodle had a bright, fancy **ruff** around its neck.

Opposite words

delicate The **delicate** cloth is trimmed with fine lace.

smooth Stir the paint until it's **smooth**.

soft Hank stroked the cat's **soft** fur.

row
  see noise

rude
  *see opposite
  of* nice

rugged
  see rough

run

rush
  see hurry

run *(verb)*

When you move your legs quickly to take you along the ground, you **run**: *Run and call for help.*

dash   I **dashed** after my grandmother, as she had forgotten her keys.

flow   The treacle **flowed** into the bowl.

hurry   You'll have to **hurry** to catch her.

race   We cheered the winner as she **raced** past the line.

sprint   Jan **sprinted** across the field like a little antelope.

trot   Horses walk, **trot**, canter, or gallop; humans walk, jog, or run.

see also hurry

S

sad (adjective)

People are **sad** when something has happened that upsets them: *Tim was **sad** when his cat died.*

depressed So many things went wrong, and we all felt **depressed**.

dismal The sunshine did not reach the **dismal** street.

gloomy Why are you so **gloomy**?

miserable I've been **miserable** without you.

sorrowful Charles Dickens wrote of the **sorrowful** plight of the poor.

unhappy Sue was **unhappy** when Simon went abroad.

Other words glum, heartbroken, tragic

Opposite words

cheerful She's a **cheerful** girl; she's always smiling.

happy We're **happy** to hear your good news.

see also funny, happy

save
 see keep

saw
 see cut

say

say *(verb)*

When you **say** something, you use your voice to make sounds, or express thoughts in writing: *I have to **say** that I enjoyed my stay here. What does the paper **say** about the weather?*

agree   I am very glad that you **agree**.

declare   I **declare** this museum open.

exclaim   "What a strange hat!" **exclaimed** Ginny.

insist   Don **insisted** that we'd met before.

pronounce How do you **pronounce** 'last'?

recite   Jack **recited** a funny poem.

remark   Dad **remarked** on the room's neatness.

reply   "Never," I heard him **reply**.

speak   I can **speak** a little Spanish.

suggest   I **suggest** we all go for a swim.

tell   Please **tell** me what's the matter!

utter   I was so surprised that I couldn't **utter** a word.

Other words announce, express, mention, murmur, mutter, shout, state, whisper, yell

scared
see afraid

scarper
see escape

seal
see shut

secure
see fast, strong

see

see *(verb)*

If we **see**, we recognize or distinguish some-thing with our eyes: *I see a group of people coming towards us. Can you see what's on the label?*

inspect   Sherlock Holmes **inspected** the letter through his magnifying glass.

notice   I **notice** that you've come on your bicycle.

observe   **Observe** how the horse moves.

peer   We **peered** through the crack.

understand Now I **understand** why you wanted to leave early.

watch   **Watch** carefully, and I'll make this box disappear!

see also look

Same sound

sea   (*noun*) The sailors were at **sea** for two weeks without seeing land.

seem
  see look

seize
  see catch, take

select
  see pick

send

send *(verb)*

To **send** is to cause something or someone to move or be moved from one place to another: *I'll **send** you a letter tomorrow. I'll **send** my brother to pick you up.*

convey   Please **convey** my best wishes to your parents.

dispatch   Colonel Briggs **dispatched** his report.

launch   The rocket was **launched** into space.

post   This letter was **posted** yesterday.

transmit   The radio operator **transmitted** a distress message immediately.

Opposite words

receive   I **received** lots of gifts on my birthday.

see also get

sense
see feel

separate
see opposite
of join

serious
see opposite
of funny

serve
see help

set
see put

severe
see opposite
of kind

shake

sharp
see opposite
of dull

shatter
see break

shiver
see shake

short
see small

shake *(verb)*

You **shake** something if you move it up and down or from side to side with short, quick movements: *Before you open the bottle, **shake** it well. The bus **shook** as it drove over the level crossing.*

flutter   We watched the flag **flutter**.

quiver   Kerry **quivered** with excitement as she entered the circus tent.

shiver   We all **shivered** with cold.

shudder   Seeing the spider in the bath made me **shudder**!

sway   Our boat **swayed** from side to side.

tremble   The thunder made the dog **tremble**.

vibrate   The building **vibrated** as the airliner swept over it.

shout
see call

show

show *(verb)*

If you allow or cause something to be seen, or make it visible, you **show** it: *Let me **show** you our garden.*

demonstrate The manager **demonstrated** the new washing machine.

display Many gifts were **displayed**.

expose My face is quite sore after being **exposed** to the wind.

indicate He spoke no English, but pointed to **indicate** what he wanted.

reveal She smiled, **revealing** a row of shining white teeth.

teach Could you **teach** me how to operate the computer?

performance *(noun)* I saw a marvellous **performance** at the opera.

Other words *(noun)* exhibition, fair, film, play

showy
see loud

shrill
see loud

shudder
see shake

shuffle
see mix

shut

shy
see quiet *and*
opposite of bold

silence
see opposite
of noise

silent
see quiet

silky
see soft

simple
see clear, plain

shut *(verb)*

If you move something to cover an opening, or place a cover on something, you **shut** it: *Please **shut** the door as you go out.*

bar We tried to cross the bridge, but a herd of cattle **barred** our way.

close **Close** your eyes and imagine you are back in the Middle Ages.

fasten Somebody had **fastened** the old chest with iron bands.

lock I've **locked** all the doors.

seal I placed the letter in an envelope and **sealed** it carefully.

closed (*adjective*) By the time we reached the town, all the shops were **closed**.

sink
  see fall *and*
  opposite of rise

sketch
  see picture

skid
  see slide

skilful
  see able

skill
  see touch

skinny
  see thin

sleek
  see smooth

sleep
  see rest

slender
  see thin

slice
  see cut

slide

slide *(verb)*

You **slide** if you move, or cause something to move, smoothly over a surface: *You don't have to push these doors; they **slide** open.*

glide   The music floated across the hall as the dancers **glided** by.

skid   I applied the brakes, and the car **skidded** on the slippery road.

slip   The soap **slipped** out of my hands.

slither   The snake **slithered** through the long grass.

slight
see small

slip
see slide

slither
see slide

slow
see opposite of fast

smack
see hit

small

small *(adjective)*

Something that is not large, is **small**: *Only a small number of people live in our village.*

little   The **little** boy has lost his dad in the crowd.

minute   [my nute] The words were so **minute** that we needed a magnifying glass to read them.

puny   In olden times, children were often **puny** because they weren't fed properly.

short   Dachshunds have **short** legs.

slight   Mary is **slight** and delicate.

tiny   We lifted a stone, and lots of **tiny** creatures scurried away.

trivial   It's not important, just a **trivial** matter.

unimportant   It's an **unimportant** flaw in the design.

Opposite words

large   We have a small house, but it has a **large** garden.

see also big

smart
  see nice

smash
  see break

smile
  see laugh

smooth

snatch
  see take

snigger
  see laugh

snip
  see cut

soak
  see wet

soar
  see rise

smooth (adjective)

When something has a surface that is free from rough parts, dents, or lumps, we say it is **smooth**: *The tide has gone out, and the sand looks **smooth**.*

even   The ship continued through the seas at an **even** speed.

flat   The land is **flat** around here, there isn't a hill for miles.

level   See how **level** the grass is after I used our new roller.

polished   That **polished** table top looks just like glass.

sleek   The panther's **sleek** fur gleams.

Other words calm, creamy, silky

Opposite words *see* rough

soft

soiled
see dirty

solid
see strong

solitary
see lonely

soothe
*see opposite
of* hurt

sorrowful
see sad

sound
see good, noise

sour
see bad

sparse
see thin

speak
see say, talk

speech
see talk

speed
see hurry

spin
see turn

soft *(adjective)*

Anything that is easy to mould, press, or dent is called **soft**: *This bed has a lovely **soft** mattress.*

delicate	What **delicate** wings butterflies have!
fluffy	The hens' eggs have hatched, and now there are dozens of **fluffy** chicks.
gentle	A warm, **gentle** breeze was blowing.
pliable	This modelling clay needs warming to make it **pliable**.
quiet	The children whispered in **quiet** voices.
silky	Her hair was soft and **silky**.

see also quiet *and opposite of* loud, rough

Opposite words *see* hard

Sport

A B C of sports

American football archery badminton baseball basketball billiards boxing canoeing cricket curling darts fencing fives high jump hockey horse riding judo karate lacrosse long jump luge netball pelota pole vault polo pool real tennis rodeo rowing Rugby running sailing shooting showjumping skating skiing snooker soccer softball squash swimming table tennis tennis tobogganing water polo water skiing wrestling

Sound the same

cricket (*game*)	cricket (*insect*)
cue (*billiard*)	queue (*line*)
bowled (*threw a ball*)	bold (*daring*)
links (*where golf is played*)	lynx (*cat-like animal*)

Pairing

Match the following three-letter groups to make six-letter words connected with sport.

kar soc ten pel box rid ski run jum arr hoc

ing ing ner ows per key ate nis cer ota ing

**Here are some main divisions of sport.
Can you group all the sports on these pages?**

combat sports (e.g. boxing)   water sports

athletics   court games

target sports   goal sports

cue sports   bat and ball games

winter sports   equestrian events

split
  see break

sprint
  see run

stand
  see put

stare
  see look

start

steal
  see take

step
  see walk

stern
  see hard

stew
  see cook

stick
  see put

stiff
  see hard

still
  see calm

stingy
  see mean

start *(verb)*

When something **starts**, it is set in motion, or happens for the first time: *I **started** a new job this morning, so I set my alarm clock to wake me up early.*

begin   The Pilgrim Fathers went to America to **begin** a new life.

commence   The show **commences** at eight o'clock.

establish We **established** our company over 40 years ago.

introduce They are going to **introduce** a new TV programme tonight.

open   The story **opens** in 1715.

Opposite words *see* end

stint
see turn

stir
see mix

stop
see opposite
of go

stormy
see rough *and*
opposite of calm

strange
see funny, odd

stretch
see pull

stride
see walk

strike
see hit

strive
see try

stroll
see walk

strong

struggle
see fight

strong *(adjective)*

If you are **strong**, you have great power and are able to do things that need energy: *In some countries, strong animals, such as oxen, are used to pull carts.*

brawny   He had large muscles on his **brawny** arms.

firm   The firefighters held on to the hose with a **firm** grip.

hardy   Farmers are tough and **hardy**.

powerful   The apes were **powerful** enough to uproot trees.

robust   The athletes are young and **robust**.

secure   Gold is stored in **secure** vaults.

solid   The house was built on **solid** rock foundations.

sturdy   That is a **sturdy** old oak tree.

tough   The mast was held in position by **tough** cables.

see also able

Other words enthusiastic, unbreakable, violent, vivid

Opposite words *see* weak

stupid
  see opposite of clever

sturdy
  see strong

suffer
  see feel

suggest
  see say

suitable
  see good, right

supply
  see give

support
  see help

suppose
  see think

sure

swallow
  see eat

swap
  see change

sway
  see shake

swift
  see fast

sure *(adjective)*

You are **sure** if you have no doubts and know something to be right: *Jack is my oldest friend, and I am **sure** he is honest and loyal.*

certain   I'm **certain** we have met before.

confident   Betsy is **confident** that she'll pass her examination.

firm   I was always **firm** in my belief that dogs are intelligent animals.

trusting   You have such a **trusting** nature and believe what people tell you.

Same sound

shore   (*noun*) It's fun to play in the rock pools along the sea **shore**.

Opposite words

distrustful Matt ran off with our money, and I'm **distrustful** of such people now.

doubtful   It's a nice bracelet, but I think its value is **doubtful**.

uncertain   He went off to Australia, and his whereabouts are **uncertain**.

T

take *(verb)*

When you **take** something, you get hold of it and possess it: *Take this book for your trip.*

bear   That bridge won't **bear** the weight of our car.

bring   **Bring** me a pound of apples from the market.

capture   The city has been **captured**.

carry   I'll **carry** these bags for you.

grasp   Jacqui **grasped** the spade and began to dig.

seize   The customs officials **seized** the smugglers as they were carrying the barrels from their boat.

snatch   The robber **snatched** her bag.

steal   Thieves broke into the safe to **steal** gold and jewels.

Other words grab, pinch

Opposite words

give   If I win, I'll **give** you half!

reject   The editor **rejected** my poems.

see also give

talented
see able, clever

talk

tap
see hit

teach
see show

telephone
see call

tell
see say, talk

tender
see kind

terminate
see end

terror
see fright

test
see try

thick
see opposite
of thin

talk *(verb)*

When we speak out loud and hold a conversation, we **talk**: *I'd like to **talk** to you about your holiday.*

chat I can **chat** for hours with Tom.

discuss I have some good ideas which I would like to **discuss** with you.

speak Austrians and many Swiss **speak** German.

tell **Tell** your friends that supper's ready.

speech *(noun)* After dinner, a well-known author made a *speech*.

thin *(adjective)*

If something is not very wide, or is not thick or fat, it is **thin**: *This vegetable soup is watery and **thin**.*

fine   This silk is so **fine** that you can hardly see the threads.

lean   Tom is a tall, **lean** boy, but his brother is quite plump.

narrow   That hole is too **narrow** even for a mouse to get through.

skinny   Bess was a **skinny** little puppy.

slender   The **slender** threads of the spider's web glittered in the sun.

sparse   This area is dry, with some **sparse** trees and bushes.

Opposite words

heavy   There was a **heavy** snowfall.

thick   All the flights have been cancelled because of **thick** fog.

thin

think

thoughtful
see nice

thoughtless
see opposite
of careful

throw away
see opposite
of keep

thrust
see push

thump
see hit

timid
see quiet *and*
opposite of bold

tiny
see small *and*
opposite of big

toast
see cook

toil
see work

think *(verb)*

If you work something out in your head, or give thought to something, you **think**: *Before I tackle any job, I like to **think** about it. I **think** I'll go to bed now.*

believe   Columbus **believed** that the world was round.

conclude   After a week with no message, we **concluded** that the ship had sunk.

consider   I **consider** this painting to be Picasso's finest work.

expect   If those clouds come near, I **expect** we'll have rain.

fancy   I **fancy** your plan won't work.

know   Do you **know** how the fire started?

suppose   I **suppose** the teacher is right.

touch

tough
  see hard, strong

trace
  see find

tranquil
  see quiet

transform
  see turn

transmit
  see send

travel
  see go

tread
  see walk

tremble
  see shake

trim
  see cut

trip
  see fall

trivial
  see small

touch *(verb)*

When you put your hands on something, or feel something, you **touch** it: *It is dangerous to* **touch** *the live wire!* You can also be **touched** if something affects your feelings: *The teacher was very* **touched** *when the children presented her with a birthday gift.* Also, the word as a *noun* means 'talent': *John is a great cook; he's got just the right* **touch**.

affect	The whole country was **affected** by the train drivers' strike.
feel	I **feel** rather cold without my woollen sweater.
finger	Please don't **finger** the grapes.
grope	It was so dark, I had to **grope** for the door handle.
handle	Don't **handle** that hot dish; use the oven gloves.

skill	(*noun*) It requires great **skill** to make clocks and watches.

see also feel

Transport

Getting About

By gondola in Venice

By wheelbarrow in China AD 300

In a Mississippi stern wheeler

By elephant in India

By balloon over Paris 1850

Car and bar

Finish off these words to find a means of getting about. The number of dashes shows the number of letters you need to make the word.

horse-drawn vehicle	car _ _ _ _ _	a small cart	bar _ _ _
goods carried by ships	car _ _	flat-bottomed boat	bar _ _
a home on wheels	car _ _ _ _	on foot without shoes	bar _ _ _ _ _

Same vehicle, different word

British	American
tram	*street car*
caravan	*trailer*
aeroplane	*airplane*
underground	*subway*
dodgem	*bumper car*
engine driver	*engineer*
bonnet	*hood*
petrol	*gasoline*
gear lever	*gear shift*
flyover	*overpass*
car park	*parking lot*
boot	*trunk*

By air   jumbo jet

By land   TGV train

By sea   hydrofoil

Sound the same

fare / *fair*

plane / *plain*

air / *heir*

sea / *see*

wheel / *we'll*

cruise / *crews*

oar / *or, ore*

pedal / *peddle*

road / *rode, rowed*

trot
see run

trusting
see sure

try

try *(verb)*

When you endeavour to do something, you **try**: *I can meet you next week, but do **try** to be early.*

aim   Tim will **aim** to play better.

attempt   The water is deep, so don't **attempt** to get in unless you can swim.

strive   Sally **strives** hard at hockey, but she's not very good.

test   All the light bulbs were **tested** before being sold.

effort   (*noun*) It required some **effort** to move the large piano.

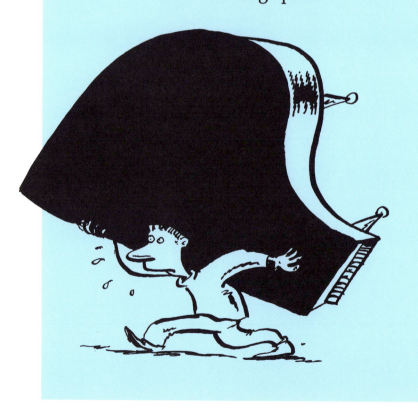

tug
see pull

tumble
see fall

turn

twist
see turn

turn (*verb*)

The word **turn** can mean several things, as in these sentences: *I shall **turn** the corner into the next street. This record player **turns** at several speeds. In autumn the leaves **turn** brown. It's my **turn** to ride the bicycle.*

change   The wizard **changed** the mice into ponies.

spin   The windmill's sails **spin** around as the wind blows.

transform   The old mill-house has been **transformed** into a cottage.

twist   As Tina drew in the kite, she **twisted** the string around a stick.

wind   Make sure you **wind** the clock before going to bed.

bend   (*noun*) Be careful, there's a sharp **bend** in the road ahead.

go   (*noun*) Julia had a **go** on the dodgems.

stint   (*noun*) We all do our **stint** in collecting cans for re-cycling.

see also change

U

ugly
see opposite of beautiful

uncertain
see opposite of sure

understand
see know, see

undo
see opposite of make

uneven
see rough

unfair
see opposite of fair

unfit
see wrong

unhappy
see sad

unimportant
see small

uninteresting
see dry

unite
see join

unkind
see mean

unoccupied
see empty

unskilled
see opposite of able

unsuitable
see wrong

unusual
see odd

upright
see right

upset
see angry, hurt

usual
see opposite of odd

utter
see say

V

vacant
see empty

vanish
see go

vary
see change

vast
see big

vibrate
see shake

visit
see call

void
see empty

W

walk *(verb)*

When we move about on foot from one place to another, we **walk**: *It's such a nice day; let's **walk** home.*

go   I **go** to school every day except Saturdays and Sundays.

hike   When the summer comes, we'll **hike** in the mountains.

march   Soldiers **marched** up the hill.

step   I have something to show you. Would you **step** this way?

stride   Martha was a strong walker, and **strode** off ahead of the rest.

stroll   We **strolled** through the woods.

tread   **Tread** carefully, there may be snakes in the long grass.

see also go

Other words
strut, tiptoe, tramp

Weather and climate

Whether the weather be hot
Or whether the weather be not,
We'll weather the weather
Whatever the weather
Whether we like it or not.

thermometer

weather vane

barometer

rain-gauge

thunder and lightning

rain

downpour

drizzle

hail

sleet

precipitation

shower

raincoat

umbrella

macintosh

wellingtons

galoshes

dry
drought
flood
thaw
freeze

It is cool fresh chilly cold bitter frosty freezing icy

It is fair fine sunny mild warm heavy muggy hot

It is damp humid dewy wet

It is misty foggy cloudy overcast murky

Sound the same
weather / *whether*

chilly / *chilli*

fair / *fare*

freeze / *frees, frieze*

hale / *hail*

mist / *missed*

rain / *reign, rein*

squall breeze wind gust gale

tempest tornado hurricane

cyclone typhoon whirlwind

137

wary
  see careful

watch
  see look, see

watchful
  see careful

water
  see wet

watery
  see weak

weak

weak *(adjective)*

Anything or anyone who is **weak** is without power or strength, and not strong: *After her illness, Jill was too **weak** to stand for long. The mooring rope was too **weak**, and the boat broke loose.*

delicate   Don't put that plate in the dishwasher; it's too **delicate**!

faint   We halted in the tunnel as we heard a **faint** sound ahead.

feeble   After being lost, our dog Rover was tired, but gave a **feeble** wag of his tail.

frail   Grandpa was quite **frail**, but happy to celebrate his birthday.

watery   You call this **watery** liquid soup?

Other words flimsy, helpless, puny

Opposite words *see* strong

wet

wet *(adjective)*

Something full of moisture, soaked in water or some other liquid, is described as **wet**: *When we were caught in the rain, our clothes got soaking **wet**.*

damp   Our shed has a leaky roof, and the inside is **damp**.

moist   There had been a heavy dew, and the ground was **moist**.

rainy   The pond is full after so many **rainy** days.

moisten   *(verb)* Sally **moistened** the flap on the envelope and stuck it down.

soak   *(verb)* These beans should be **soaked** in water for two hours.

water   *(verb)* **Water** the seeds well.

see also opposite of dry

Opposite words

arid   The land was **arid**, almost like a desert.

dry   Our washing has been outside for hours and is quite **dry**.

parched   We've walked for miles, and our throats are **parched**.

see also dry

wicked
 see wrong

wide
 see big

win
 see get

wind
 see turn

withdraw
 see opposite of put

withhold
 see opposite of give

work

work out
 see find

work *(noun)*

Something that needs effort to do or complete is called **work**: *It took a lot of **work**, but we have finished making our garden.*

effort Steve had several tries and managed to jump the fence after a great **effort**.

employment The new factory gave **employment** to many local people.

job On Saturdays I help with **jobs** around the house.

labour Building the Eiffel Tower needed the **labour** of hundreds of workers.

operate *(verb)* Our television is old, but it **operates** well.

toil *(verb)* Coal miners **toil** each day below the ground.

Other words business, occupation, profession, trade

worn
see old

worship
see love

wound
see hurt

wrong

Y

yell
see call

young
see opposite of old

wrong (adjective)

This word has two main meanings. If something is not right or correct, it is **wrong**: *Tom got all his sums **wrong**.* Also, it means 'evil': *People who do **wrong** are sent to prison. It is **wrong** to tell lies.*

false   People once thought that the Earth was flat, but this is **false**.

incorrect   You have failed the spelling test because all your answers were **incorrect**.

mistaken   I thought the telephone number was 371226, but I was **mistaken**.

unfit   This old typewriter must be scrapped, as it's **unfit** for use.

unsuitable The road ahead is uneven and **unsuitable** for traffic.

wicked   There have been many **wicked** people in history.

Opposite words

correct   'Pharaoh' and 'siege' are the **correct** spellings.

proper   Tracey has had **proper** training to use the word processor.

right   Is this the **right** road for St. Petersburg?

Same sound, different meaning

A homonym is a word which has the same sound and spelling as another but a different meaning: for example, *seal* meaning 'to shut' and *seal*, the animal. A homograph is a word with the same spelling as another but with a different meaning and sometimes a different sound: for example, *bow* meaning a ribbon and *bow* meaning to bend. A homophone is a word with the same sound as another word, but a different spelling: for example *bear*, the animal and *bare* meaning not covered by clothes.
Here is a list of some more homophones:

adds	adze	coarse	course	idle	idol
ail	ale	cord	chord	in	inn
allowed	aloud	cue	queue	its	it's
altar	alter	daze	days	knew	new
band	banned	dear	deer	knot	not
be	bee	dew	due	know	no
beat	beet	earn	urn	laze	lays
berth	birth	fair	fare	leak	leek
blew	blue	find	fined	lesson	lessen
boar	bore	fir	fur	lute	loot
boy	buoy	for	fore, four	lynx	links
brake	break	graze	greys	maid	made
buy	by	heard	herd	main	mane
cannon	canon	hear	here	meat	meet
ceiling	sealing	him	hymn	mind	mined
choose	chews	hoard	horde	muscle	mussel
clause	claws	holy	wholly	need	knead

none	nun	rack	wrack	son	sun
nose	knows	read	reed	steal	steel
ode	owed	real	reel	sweet	suite
our	hour	red	read	tail	tale
pain	pane	right	write	tease	teas, tees
past	passed	road	rowed	their	there
patience	patients	rose	rows	to	two, too
peace	piece	sail	sale	turn	tern
place	plaice	scene	seen	vain	vein
peer	pier	seam	seem	waist	waste
plain	plane	seize	seas, sees	wood	would
praise	prays, preys	slay	sleigh	yoke	yolk
presence	presents	some	sum	you	ewe

Answers

The community's helping hands

church	priest
synagogue	rabbi
fire station	firefighter
hospital	nurse, doctor, dentist
school	teacher
post office	postman, postwoman
kitchen	cook
police station	policeman, policewoman
railway station	train driver

Containers
Double words vessel, can, sack, sink

Family
Man and woman at a party: the boy is the nephew of the man's wife.

Family problems grandfather (Mr Bowles), sister (Mrs Jones), son (Winston), cousin (Deri), your grandfather

Houses
Double words shed, flat, yard, way

Parts of a house window, door, chimney, roof/room, floor, wall, ceiling, stairs

Odd one out The Tower of Babel, because the others are still standing.

Land
Hidden rivers Nile, Hudson, Tigris

What animal lives where?

camel	desert
kangaroo	bush
eagle	cliff
cattle	plain
squirrel	woods
dolphin	sea

Music
Musical groups
strings: harp, violin, cello, guitar, double bass **woodwind**: clarinet, oboe **brass**: trumpet, trombone **percussion**: xylophone, tambourine, gong

Plants
Fruit, flower, vegetable or tree?
fruit: pear, apple, grape, avocado, nut, pineapple, lemon **flower**: lily, tulip, iris, daffodil, daisy, nasturtium **vegetable**: lettuce, onion, carrot, bean, pea, celery, cauliflower, cassava **tree**: pear, elm, apple, beech, oak

Roots geranium, tulip, daisy, dandelion, chrysanthemum, sunflower, marigold, wallflower

Sport
Pairing karate, soccer, tennis, pelota, boxing, riding, skiing, runner, jumper, arrows, hockey

Divisions of sport
combat sports: boxing, fencing, judo, karate, wrestling **athletics**: high jump, long jump, pole vault, running **target sports**: archery, darts, shooting **cue sports**: billiards, pool, snooker **winter sports**: curling, luge, skating, skiing, tobogganing **water sports**: canoeing, rowing, sailing, swimming, water polo, water skiing **court games**: badminton, basketball, fives, netball, real tennis, squash, tennis **goal sports**: American football, hockey, lacrosse, Rugby, soccer **bat and ball games**: baseball, cricket, softball, squash, table tennis, tennis **equestrian events**: horse riding, polo, rodeo, showjumping

Transport
carriage, cargo, caravan, barrow, barge, barefoot